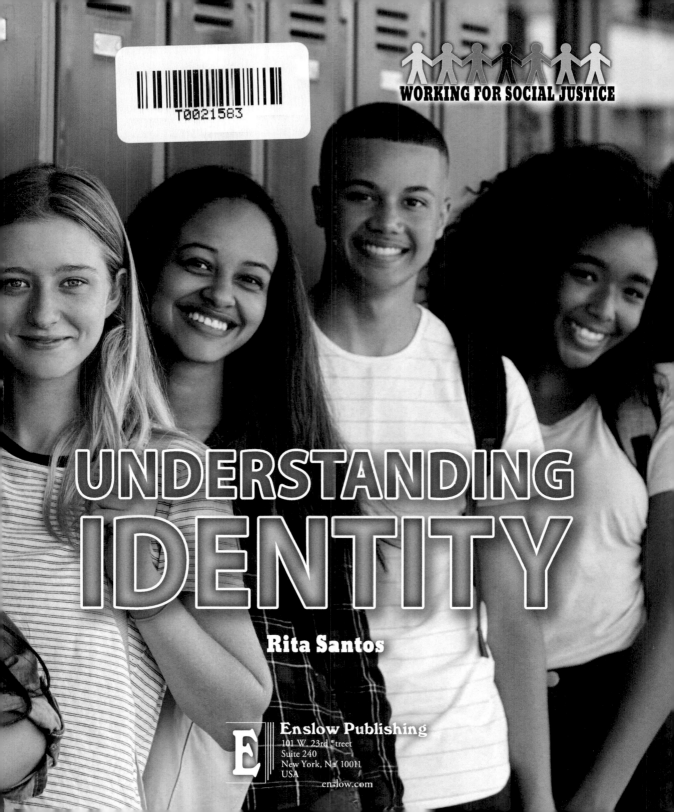

WORKING FOR SOCIAL JUSTICE

UNDERSTANDING IDENTITY

Rita Santos

Enslow Publishing
101 W. 23rd Street
Suite 240
New York, NY 10011
USA
enslow.com

Published in 2020 by Enslow Publishing, LLC.
101 W. 23rd Street, Suite 240, New York, NY 10011

Library of Congress Cataloging-in-Publication Data

Names: Santos, Rita, author.
Title: Understanding identity / Rita Santos.
Description: New York : Enslow Publishing, 2020 | Series: Working for social justice | Audience: Grade level 3-6. | Includes bibliographical references and index.
Identifiers: LCCN 2018050241| ISBN 9781978507876 (library bound) | ISBN 9781978508040 (pbk.) | ISBN 9781978508057 (6 pack)
Subjects: LCSH: Identity (Psychology)—Juvenile literature. | Ethnicity—Juvenile literature. | Race—Juvenile literature.
Classification: LCC BF697 .S2467 2020 | DDC 305—dc23

LC record available at https://lccn.loc.gov/2018050241

Printed in the United States of America

To Our Readers: We have done our best to make sure all website addresses in this book were active and appropriate when we went to press. However, the author and the publisher have no control over and assume no liability for the material available on those websites or on any websites they may link to. Any comments or suggestions can be sent by email to customerservice@enslow.com.

Photo Credits: Cover, pp. 1, 26 Monkey Business Images/Shutterstock.com; p. 5 DGLimages/Shutterstock.com; p. 8 © iStockphoto.com/ajaykampani; p. 10 Geartooth Productions/Shutterstock.com; pp. 11, 16 pixelheadphoto digitalskillet/ Shutterstock.com; p. 14 Lopolo/Shutterstock.com; p. 18 MJTH/Shutterstock.com; pp. 20, 29 Rawpixel.com/Shutterstock. com; p. 21 YaniSinla/Shutterstock.com; p. 22 Little Pig Studio/Shutterstock.com; p. 25 Cultura Motion/Shutterstock.com; cover graphics Stankovic/Shutterstock.com.

CONTENTS

INTRODUCTION

When you belong to a club at school, it means you share at least one thing in common with the other people in the club. If you're a part of the chess club, it means you all enjoy chess. Everything else about you may seem different, but you're all still chess players. Having something be a part of your identity is like being in a club with other people who share that identity.

But just because you're all chess players doesn't mean you're *only* chess players. You could also be a soccer player or a debate team captain or a student of mixed martial arts. In the same way that you can belong to many clubs, you have many identities. Your identity can include your hobbies and skills, and your race, ethnicity, gender, religion, and sexual orientation. Our identities help shape how we view the world and how the world views us. In some situations, our identities can help us. They can make us feel like we're part of a community. But some people face intolerance because of one or more of their identities. By learning about the many identities people have and how those different identities affect their lives, we can help fight intolerance in our communities.

Having a quality or trait that is part of your identity is like belonging to a club in school.

Understanding our identity is important because it helps us make the best choices for ourselves. Learning about what our strengths and weaknesses are can help us make a plan to do our best. Part of understanding our identity is learning what our values are. It helps us decide how we want to treat others.

The path to understanding our identity sounds like a lot of work, but it's actually a lot of fun! Every time we try something new, whether we enjoy it or not, it teaches us something about ourselves.

WHO ARE YOU?

one

There are many different kinds of cookies in the world. While a peanut butter cookie and a chocolate chip cookie may taste very different, their recipes are basically the same. Only a few ingredients separate a chocolate chip cookie from a peanut butter cookie. Human identity works in a similar way.

WHAT IS IDENTITY?

Your **identity** is everything that makes you you! It's the recipe that makes you who you are. It's the things you like and dislike. It's also things like where you're from or the color of your hair. Everything from your race to your sex and gender are a part of your identity. Your identity is unique. You may share parts of your identity with other people but no one else is exactly like you.

Followers of the Sikh religion wear physical garments that express their faith.

Some parts of our identity, like our physical features, are easy to see. Other parts, like believing in a religion, aren't apparent just by looking at people. People who follow the Sikh religion may choose to wear a turban. They are using their clothing to show a part of their identity that is important to them but otherwise not visible to others. It is a sign they are proud of that part of themselves. It's also a way for them to find other people who share that identity.

INTERSECTIONALITY

Because our identities are made up of so many things, no one has just one identity. Everyone belongs to many different groups based on the different identities they have.

Sometimes we can have more than one of the same kind of identity. For example, someone who was born in the United States but whose parents emigrated from India has an American identity and an Indian identity. This person has two ethnic identities. A person with a white mother and a black father would have two racial identities.

Because people have many different parts to their identities we can usually find that we have something in common with almost everyone we meet.

Our identity impacts how we treat others and how they treat us. The way the various parts of our personal identity combine also affects how we

Social Constructs

Some parts of our identity, like our height, are based on facts that can be scientifically proven. But other parts are known as social constructs, which are basically the ideas society has about a certain topic. Gender is a good example. Many traits associated with gender, like hairstyle or clothing, are given meaning by a society. The idea that girls, not boys, should wear dresses is not based on anything biological or medical. It is just what society has believed to be proper.

Social constructs fit many people but not everyone. We are all allowed to construct our own identities in any way we choose.

The idea that boys or girls can only wear a certain kind of clothing is a social construct.

If children have a white parent and a black parent, both of these backgrounds make up their racial identity.

experience the world. A black man and a white man may share the experience of being male, but their racial experience is different. Imagine if each part of your identity was a street. The places where the streets connect are called intersections. When we discuss the ways the parts of our identities connect, it's called **intersectionality**. It's important for us to understand the ways our identities intersect and how those intersections affect us. But first, let's look at where identities come from.

two

Where Our Identity Comes From

Our identity comes from many parts of our life. Some of these parts, like the town you were born in or your race, aren't chosen by you. These are parts of our identity we're usually unable to change. But some parts of our identity, like being part of a sports team, are chosen. The things we like may change over time. The toys you liked as a baby are probably different from the toys you like now. This is a normal part of growing, and healthy humans are always growing. As our likes and interests change over time, so do certain parts of our identity.

The things we enjoy, like music, can be a part of our identity.

Choosing Our Values

An important part of our identity comes from our **values**. Values are made up of what we think is important in life, like spending time with our families, and how we think people should behave. Our values are often influenced by people close to us, like our parents or teachers. When people have a positive influence over others they're called **role models**.

When we're choosing our values, it's important to make sure we're only taking them from positive

Self-Concept

Though you probably don't remember it, at around eighteen months old, you came to understand that you were a person: you started to form a self-concept. Your self-concept is the idea you have of who you are. It's made up of your self-image, which is how you see yourself, and your self-esteem, which is how you feel about yourself. Your self-concept isn't always accurate. People with eating disorders may have a self-image of weighing more than they really do. When people's self-concept is different from reality, talking to a therapist can help them get a more realistic view of themselves.

Parents, guardians, and teachers play an important role in shaping our values.

sources. TV shows and movies can have a big influence on how people feel about themselves. But there is a lack of **diversity** in most media. This means most characters look similar and have similar ethnic or racial backgrounds. Having a lack of diversity sends the message that only people who look a certain way are important. But in reality, how you look matters less than how you treat others. A good role model makes us feel good about ourselves without putting anyone else down.

Talking About Ourselves

We use words to describe everything around us, including ourselves. The words we use to tell each other what identities we belong to are sometimes called **labels**. A label like "cisgender" lets others know that our gender identity matches the gender we were assigned at birth, while the label "transgender" lets others know that our gender identity may be different from the gender assigned to us. Labels can help us quickly describe a part of ourselves to others. Labels can help people to feel like their identities are understood by the people who care about them. Labels can also help us find others who share our identity.

However, labels, like all words, can also be used to hurt people. Words can help us feel more connected. But we can also use words to hurt each other. When people use a mean or unkind label to hurt a certain community, the label becomes offensive. It's similar

Learning who we are and establishing a healthy self-image and identity are part of growing up.

to a bully who uses name calling to make others feel bad. Continuing to use a word that a community finds offensive is a form of bullying. Labels work best when they are chosen by the people they are describing.

three

Our Identity and the World

Having different identities means we belong to some groups of people and not others. This is because we a part of a diverse world, where there are many different types of people. When the majority of people in your community share a part of your identity, you are a part of the majority. When a part of your identity is less commonly shared in your community, it makes you a minority.

How We Treat Each Other

There is nothing wrong with being a part of a majority or minority group. Diversity makes the world a more interesting place. However, some people are **intolerant** of other people's identity. Some people who are intolerant dislike those who are different from them. Many intolerant people

People of different racial or ethnic backgrounds often have different experiences of the world, but we can still understand and appreciate each other.

simply don't know much about people who aren't like them. Unfortunately, their lack of understanding means they treat people with other identities badly. This also means that people experience the world differently based on their identities.

When people are treated badly because of a part of their identity, it's called **discrimination**. Some people

Internet Identities

Most people know it's wrong to make fun of other people. We know being a bully is wrong. Some people think it's okay to say mean things to people online if they're strangers. But a cruel name stings no matter whom or where it comes from. Who we are online is a reflection of who we are in the real world. A bully is a bully even if they're only mean online.

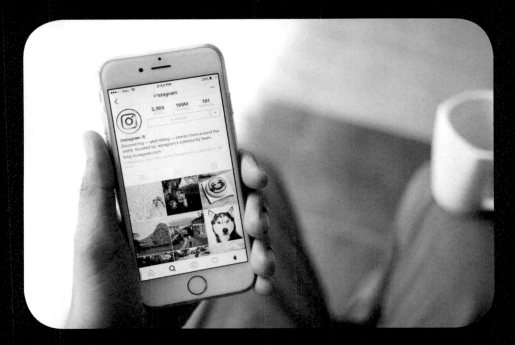

While social media can be a fun way of sharing things with friends, some use these platforms to bully or shame others.

are more likely to face certain types of discrimination than others. People who belong to minority groups are often the target of discrimination because they are seen as different from the majority.

Negative stereotypes have led to discrimination against women trying to succeed in male-dominated fields, like math and science.

Discrimination is always wrong, but it's also a common problem in our society.

People can face discrimination for some parts of their identity but not others. An American Christian black woman may be discriminated against because of her race or her gender. But because Christianity is the largest religion in the United States, it's unlikely she would face religious discrimination.

How Discrimination Affects Us

The way people treat us affects how we feel about ourselves. When people are discriminated against it makes them feel bad about their identity. This is unfair. Intolerance can cause people to believe things about themselves or other groups that aren't true. For many years, many people believed that women were not as good at math or science as men. These beliefs made women less likely to study math and science. It also made it harder for women to get jobs in math and science fields. But scientists who study gender have found that neither gender is better at math or science than the other.

Because of this false belief that women were not as good at science, women were excluded from important jobs, which meant fewer people were working toward new discoveries. When everyone is allowed to participate, scientists can solve problems faster. Every piece of identity brings a new way to think about problems. When we work together, we can do things none of us can do alone.

four

RESPECTING ALL IDENTITIES

People should be proud of who they are. We all have value. Everyone has something unique to contribute to the world. Some people think being proud of something means thinking it's the best. But pride isn't about being better than others. It's about being happy with ourselves and our accomplishments.

Talking and listening to one another is an easy way to develop understanding and empathy.

Concepts like "black pride" and the celebration of black excellence came about because of the historic discrimination and oppression of black citizens in America.

Pride should come from your success, not others' failures. When we are proud of our identities, we show respect for the identities of others.

HAVING EMPATHY

If we want to treat other people's identities with respect, we need to understand them first. Because

Why We Have Black Pride

During slavery, millions of African people were kidnapped and brought to the United States as slaves. Families were intentionally separated, which made it impossible for people to pass down their family histories. This included the countries they were originally from. So, while the descendants of European immigrants were able to pass their ethnic pride to their children, African slaves were not. Today, many black people choose to use the phrase "black pride" to honor their ethnic roots and family histories that were lost to the horrors of slavery.

of all the different pieces that make up a person's identity, everyone's life experience is different. Learning about other people's experiences can help us understand them better. Intolerance often comes from a lack of understanding. When we do our best to understand how other people's intersectionality affects them, we can help fight intolerance. When we're able to put ourselves in someone else's shoes and imagine how they might feel in a situation, it's called having **empathy**.

Having empathy makes it easier for us to care about others. When we empathize with another person, we understand that their needs and feelings are just as important as our own. Learning about the challenges others face makes it easier to notice discrimination when it happens to others. Fighting discrimination is like fighting a bully. You can win on your own, but it's much easier to stop a bully when everyone in the class finds their behavior unacceptable. If we want to ensure that everyone's identity is treated with respect, we have to let our friends know intolerance of others isn't acceptable. It's okay to dislike people who don't treat us well. It's not okay to dislike people just because of their identity.

A LIFELONG JOB

Learning who we are is a lifelong lesson. You are never too old to learn something new about yourself. As we grow up, everyone has to make choices about their lives. We choose what city we want to live in.

If we are open to learning about each other's identities, we will be much more likely to connect and form friendships.

We decide if we want to get married. We choose a job. All of these choices are easier when we understand ourselves. Our dreams and goals for ourselves are also an important part of our identity. We share so many different parts of ourselves with other people. Finding out all the ways we are alike and different is something we can enjoy doing our whole lives.

Words to Know

discrimination The unfair treatment of people based on something they cannot control, like their race or sexual orientation.

diversity When things are different from each other.

empathy The ability to put ourselves in someone else's shoes and understand how they feel.

identity Who we are as a person; it's made up of our likes and dislikes as well as the groups we belong to.

intersectionality The ways the different parts of our identities connect to each other.

intolerant Disliking people from other communities just because they have appearances or beliefs that are different from your own.

labels The words we use to describe ourselves and others.

role models People we admire and base our behavior on.

values The things we think are important in life.

LEARN MORE

Books

Manushkin, Fran. *Happy in Our Skin*. Somerville, MA:
    Candlewick, 2018.

McMeans, Julia. *Justice in Our Society* (Civic Values). New York,
    NY: Cavendish, 2018.

Mirza, Sandrine. *People of Peace: Meet 40 Amazing Activists*.
    London, UK: Wide Eyed Editions, 2018.

Websites

Kids Against Bullying

pacerkidsagainstbullying.org

This site inspires students to take action against bullying in their schools.

Race Project Kids

understandingrace.org/kids.html

Understand what it's like to walk in someone else's shoes at the Race Project.

Teaching Tolerance

splcenter.org/teaching-tolerance

Learn more about the fight to end discrimination.

INDEX

B
black pride, 27
bullying, 18, 21, 28

C
cisgender label, 17

D
discrimination, 20,
    22–23, 28
diversity, 16, 19

E
empathy, 26–28
ethnicity, 4, 9, 16, 27

G
gender, 4, 7, 10, 17, 23

H
hobbies, 4

I
identity
    respecting, 25–29
    understanding, 4–6
    what it is, 7–12
    where it comes from,
        13–18

and the world, 19–24
intersectionality, 9–12, 27
intolerance, 5, 19, 23,
    27, 28

L
labels, 17–18

M
majority, 19, 22
minority, 19, 22

P
pride, 25–26

R
race, 4, 7, 13, 23
religion, 4, 8, 23
role models, 15, 17

S
self-concept, 15
sexual orientation, 4
Sikhs, 8–9
slavery, 29
social constructs, 10

T
transgender label, 17

V
values, 15–17